…It's easy to question the status quo
When you move with the flow
Of a popular cause.
It's harder by far
When the tide is against you
To stand as a rebel without applause…

For Chrissie,
Who has brought healing
To a heart seven tenths hidden,
And for Joseph, Aaron and Anna,
The most precious gifts
I have ever received.

REBEL
without
APPLAUSE

Gerard Kelly

MINSTREL
Eastbourne

Text and front cover cartoons by Russell Davies

BRITISH LIBRARY CATALOGUING IN PUBLICATION DATA

Gerard Kelly
Rebel without applause.
I. Title
821.914

ISBN 1-85424-132-X

Printed in Great Britain for
Minstrel, an imprint of Monarch Publications Ltd
1 St Anne's Road, Eastbourne, E Sussex BN21 3UN by
BPCC Hazell Books, Aylesbury, Bucks
Typeset by Watermark, Norfolk House, Cromer

Introduction

This collection of sixty-nine poems represents the author's work during the past few years. Some of the pieces have been commissioned for use in specific settings and events, others are 'shirt-box poems', scribbled on whatever scraps of paper came to hand in the midst of a busy life.

The poems are arranged more or less alphabetically for ease of access. Around a third of them have been written particularly for a young audience, and about half the total collection are suitable for live performance of some sort.

Gerard Kelly is a youth worker with Youth For Christ, based in Exeter. His work involves contact with young people in schools and in church groups as well as a wider cross section of church congregations. In recent years poetry has formed an increasing part of his work, particularly in school assemblies, church services and youth meetings, with an emphasis on bringing together truth and humour. As well as poetry and general youth work, Gerard is also involved in a fair amount of preaching and teaching. He has performed at Spring Harvest and Greenbelt, at National Youth For Christ events and in a number of Bath revues. Gerard is married to Chrissie, and they have three children: Joseph, Aaron and Anna.

The poem 'Modern Romance' was awarded third prize in the 1988 Orbis 'Rhyme Revival' International Poetry Competition.

Contents

BEHOLD I STAND

When the night is deep
With the sense of Christmas
And expectancy hangs heavy
On every breath,
Behold, I stand at the door and knock.

When the floor is knee deep
In discarded wrapping paper
And the new books are open at page one
And the new toys are already broken,
Behold, I stand at the door and knock.

When the family is squashed
Elbow to elbow
Around the table
And the furious rush for food is over
And the only word that can describe the feeling
Is full,
Behold, I stand at the door and knock.

And when Christmas is over
And the television is silent
For the first time in two days
And who sent which card to whom
Is forgotten until next year,
Behold, I stand at the door.

And when the nation has finished celebrating
Christmas without Christ
A birthday
Without a birth
The coming of a kingdom
Without a King
And when I am
Forgotten
Despised
Rejected
Crucified —

Behold, I stand.

BOOM TOWN

I   Boom Town Rap

Twenty years I've lived
In the town of my birth,
But I still
Can't call it my own:
Since the dollar and the yen
And the property men
Are buying it,
Stone by stone.

Young local families
Can't afford homes,
Though the town has been home
All their lives.
Streets of local businesses
Fold for new offices
And dress shops
For the badminton wives.

It's a Boom Town
Boom Town:
Sick of living
In a Boom Town, Gloom Town.
The poor are dying
In this Doom Town, Tomb Town:

Need a bomb
Under this Boom Town,
BOOM town....

The rest of the wide world
Could fall down and die
For all the difference
That it makes:
Bubble of prosperity,
Cocooned from reality,
How long will it be
Until it breaks?

In a city of fine houses,
Homelessness increases,
Young people opting
To live in a tent;
Rejects of society
Looking for community –
A word often spoken
But hardly ever meant.

When you're living
In a Boom Town
Boom Town.
The poor are dying
In this Gloom Town, Tomb Town,
Need a bomb
Under this Boom Town,
BOOM town....

BOOM TOWN

II   Hearts of Stone

In my childhood
These buildings were black:
Thick with fifty years
Of carbon poison.
Soft Georgian flesh
Wearing progress
Like a cancer.
Behind their painted, flaking
Window sashes,
Widows lived
And students
And couples, starting out.
The toilets
Were on landings
And a hall table collected
Circulars
For tenants
Who had moved or died.

And then they found a way
To clean them:
Poured water on stone
For weeks on end.

Like an architectural alchemy,
The City was golden again:
Bedsits ripped out,
Widows and students rehoused
As one by one
The great houses were restored.
A population more fitting
For clean stone moved in,
To fitted bathrooms
And small bedrooms
And entryphones protecting
The hall table.

A crumbling City
Revived again.
A lost heritage
Discovered again.
Museum pieces
Dusted again.
And the poor
Displaced again.
Did a City
In need of a facelift
Have to have
A heart transplant too?

BOOM TOWN

III   Change

There are places
In this City
That we say haven't changed:
The lawns and obelisk
In Queen Square,
The view to the Crescent
Across Victoria Park,
The litter of deck chairs
Around the Parade Gardens bandstand.
No developer's lorries here,
To cart off yesterday.
No road schemes and car parks,
No glass and steel
To set on edge
A wide-eared Prince's teeth.

We think of these
As static places,
Places of refuge
When change overwhelms us.

And we don't notice
That the grass dances

Through a dizzy choreography of change.
That the trees
Grind on like juggernauts,
From sapling youth
Through spreading middle age,
To twisted pensioning.
That the soil itself
Is daily rearranged
By sinking rains
And passing worms.

These changes
We miss.
Accustomed as we are to escaping
The changes that bring death,
We forget
The changes that are life.

BOOM TOWN

IV Window Shopping

If you look at it for long enough
You can almost believe that it's real
And your reflection
In the plate glass
Makes you part of it.

'Available today on easy terms the
suite is pure hide see a full range
of CD players in our electrical
department the appliance of science
can you bear to live without satellite
TV?'

You are almost persuaded to forget
That like Dodge City
At the Saturday Matinee
This is just a facade,
That behind it
Refugees huddle for shelter
And queue for charity,
Children die from diarrhoea
And work with homicidal pesticides
And live in concrete boxes,

Whole communities
Share one tap
And mothers feed their young
On powdered death...
And the face of the Earth erupts
With scabs and scars and sores
Until there is little
Clean skin left.

But the display is backed by heavy curtains
To block unwanted light,
And if you look at it for long enough
You can almost believe that it's real:
Your reflection
In the plate glass
Makes you
Part of it.

BOOM TOWN

V   Ad Nauseum

They don't shout at you
These days
In crowded squares.
They don't hang their wares
From aprons
And fight through the crush
To accost you.
There is no cackle
Of hens,
No bleating of goats,
No clink, clink, clink
Of money counted.

These days
They rent the sides of buildings
And scream at you from posters
The size of skies.
They make neon signs
To render moonlight anaemic,
And leave their wares
To swim about
In pools of floodlit showrooms.
They hold their tongues,

Say nothing:
Yet fill your head
Your life
Your city
With the fevered volume
Of their hawking.

Modern-day money-changers
Dealers
Hustlers
Abusers of silence
In God's green temple:
But who should we look to
In this after-Messiah age,
To make a whip
And turn the tables on them?

BUCKINGHAM PALACE

They're dropping their guard
At Buckingham Palace:
I heard it all
From a maid named Alice.
She knew the sizes
Of all Di's frocks,
'I can show you the sock shop
Where she shops for socks!'
Said Alice.

They're dropping their guard
At Buckingham Palace:
A whole new ball game,
According to Alice,
'They used to be as private
As a Papal string vest:
Now they get more exposure
Than Schwarzenegger's chest,'
Said Alice.

They're dropping their guard
At Buckingham Palace:
But it's no bed of roses,
You ask Alice,
'Being Royal's hard enough,
But these days they have to cope
With also being stars
Of the world's greatest soap,'
Said Alice.

CITY TO CITY

Jim
Was a juvenile fan of football,
In his braces,
Doc Martens and jeans.
A once-a-week,
Hard-as-nails,
Do-'em-in boot boy,
He kicked his way
Through his teens.

He said
It's the survival of the fittest;
Keep yer end up,
Or you'll end up dead.
There's no time
To be soft on a stranger
When your boot's
On its way
To 'is 'ead.

At college
Jim studied Big Business
And learnt
To be charming and witty.
He landed a top job

In takeovers
And was soon a big name
In the City.

But Jim's not surprised
By his good fortune
In the Corporate Finance Game;
It's a long way
From aggro to affluence,
But the basic approach
Is the same.

COCKTAIL CONVERSATION

If I pretend
That you're noble,
Will you agree
That I'm kind?
If I act as if
I'm talking about you
But talk about me,
Would you mind?
If I take your bait
About a fascinating job
And don't challenge what you do,
Will you fall for my line
About noisy coloured neighbours
And say
That you'd have moved too?
Will you confirm
All my convictions
If I don't notice
Your assumptions are absurd?
If so
We can talk like this for hours
Without meaning
A single word.

COLOSSAL CONSUMER CHRISTMAS

It's a colossal consumer Christmas,
We'll spend record-breaking amounts:
But our thoughts are only of ourselves
When we say
It's the thought that counts.

How much is a jumper in Wool worth?
Does your Mother really Care?
If we discovered a new Super Drug,
Would the two-thirds world get their Share?

We'll give you full Marks for your Spend, Sir,
So where will your Body Shop Next?
You can be sure your credit repayments
Will be Retail-Price-Indexed.

It's a colossal consumer Christmas,
We'll spend record-breaking amounts:
But our thoughts are only of ourselves
When we say
It's the thought that counts.

Check out the crush at the check-out!
Shoppers look for a Safeway through.
Some block the Gateway: the rest go to Tesco,

You'll just have to B patient and Q.

They're going insane down at Sainsburys,
At Bejams they've jammed every till.
You won't be laughing all the way to the bank:
But you can bet your Boots that they will!

It's a colossal consumer Christmas,
We'll spend record-breaking amounts:
But our thoughts are only of ourselves
When we say
It's the thought that counts.

CONSCRIPTION

White boy
On an armoured truck
In white man's uniform:
Face as fresh as morning,
White
As christening gown.
First time in a township,
First time with a gun,
In the name of Law and Order
Come to damp
The fires down.

Brings the only Law he knows,
Law of separation;
His only Order
The order of the bullet.
Divine Nation is the rifle,
Race Hatred the trigger:
But you have to have the white boy
There to pull it.

White eyes
Of fear and menace,
Fear on black faces,
He's learnt to see Communists

At every turn.
He calls them blacks, not people,
Settlements,
Not homes:
Bulldoze the revolution,
Watch the shanties burn.

Brings the only Law he knows,
Law of separation;
His only Order
The order of the bullet.
Divine Nation is the rifle,
Race Hatred the trigger:
But you have to have the white boy
You have to have the white boy
You have to have the white boy
There to pull it.

CREATION AFFIRMATION

I love the very thought of heaven:
Where angels sing,
In perfect, perpetual choir practice.
Where Father, Son and Spirit
Rule, unchallenged,
And are honoured in full measure.
I love the very thought of heaven:
But I was not made
To live there.

I was not made
To walk on clouds,
And bask eternally
In immaterial splendour.
I was made for this green planet:
This tight ball
Of infinite beauty,
Alive with the unending possibilities
Of his creative power.
I was made for the sunshine
That blazes through the veins of leaves,
And glints on the tiny, perfect back
Of a ladybird, crossing my arm.
I was made to be human
In this most human of environments.

I was made for earth:
The earth is my home.

That's why I'm glad
That God, more than anyone,
Is a Friend of the Earth.
Prepared as he was
To die for its restoration.
And that's why I'm glad
That the magnificent, jewelled foundations
Of the mighty pearly gates,
Will be anchored
Deeply and for ever
In the soil of earth.

THE CRITIC

He wanted a Jesus
For the twentieth-century flocks,
A saviour fit
To be a superstar.
He left miracles and faith
On the cutting-room floor:
But his Gospel
Was abridged too far....

A CURE FOR THE COMMON CULT

If the Moonies
Take your money
And Sri Bagwam
Takes your mind,
If Divine Light
Leaves you in darkness
And Scientology
Leaves you blind,
If broken families
And broken lives
Are the products
Of their sacred texts:
Then it must be true
As I've heard it said,
That there's no such thing
As safe sects.

DEAL

If I love you now
A dependent
Week-old child,

Will you care for me
When I am a dependent
Weak old man?

DISCO MOTTO

As they've learnt
In Soho,
Amsterdam and Rio,
Through stereo,
Disco,
Radio and video:
A fool and his money
Are soon partied.

DISSIDENT VOICE

I lived at peace with my conscience,
Until it became
A dissident voice
In my conversation.
It was an undesirable element
In my otherwise peaceful regime,
An enemy of my state
Of independence.
Its activities destabilised
My whole economy,
And it was clearly a threat
To rational security.

At first I simply banned it
From appearing in public;
I put it under house-arrest
And allowed it no visitors.
But it would not desist
From its self-appointed role
As watch-dog to my thinking and behaviour.
So I did as any autocrat would do,
I locked it up
And threw away the key.
I sentenced it to life
In solitary confinement

And put it in a place
Where even foreign journalists
Wouldn't think to look.

But the horrors of the world
Have increasingly been lobbying my senses
Petitions of hungry children
Have been delivered to my eyes
Compassion and responsibility
Have been dripping
Through the growing hole
In my ozone layer
I am under mounting pressure
For an amnesty.

Consciences,
Like prisoners
Are never quite forgotten.

ECOLOGY TAUTOLOGY

I thought that modern industry
Had nothing new to teach me
About ecology
And the world of the soil.
But I learned from a tanker
When somebody sank her
That birds of a feather
Stick to oil.

EMPTY WORDS

When you've been on the couch
With Anne Diamond
And touched Terry Wogan's knee,
When you've laughed with Frost
On Sunday
And frowned with Day and Dimbleby,
When you've flirted by night
With Michael Aspel
And cavorted with Kilroy by day,
Then you've done all that's asked
Of a celebrity:
You've proved
You've got nothing to say.

THE ENEMY WITHIN

It's not another Blitz over London,
And it's no match for the Nazi threat:
But there's danger of historic proportions
In the rise of credit debt.
It may not be the Battle of Britain,
But it is, for the second time, true,
That never before has so much
Been owed
By so many
To so few.

THE FIRST TIME

The first time we met,
I was in costume
As Doctor Kildare
And you wore a suit
Designed for the occasion.

When you made
Your first entrance,
And your strong voice
Filled the theatre,
Your tiny figure
Made the time and place
Seem huge.
And though we kept
A kind of silence,
In our hearts
Applause thundered.

Our first kiss
Was through a mask,
And though I felt
Only gauze,
I could smell
Your soft skin.

The first time I spoke your name,
You said nothing,
But looked for me,
Trusting.

And in that moment,
I tied my life to yours
With a vow as strong as marriage.
And in that steel
And sterile room,
Cluttered
With the scrap-store sculptures
Of the birth machines,
I held,
For the first time,
My daughter.

THE FORTUNES OF NIGEL

Nigel
Was never very popular
With banks:
They kept asking him
To be more prudent.
So it came as a shock to him
To find how much they liked him
The very instant
That he became
A student.

They offered him the world
To open an account:
A free filofax
And all the extras with it.
There were discounts
On LPs,
T shirts, tapes, CDs,
There was even
A free twenty pounds credit.

So Nigel responded
As only he could:
He opened new accounts
With ALL the banks.

They seemed pleased
To have his custom,
And since he'd planned
Not to trust them,
He simply took all that they offered,
And said thanks.

But he didn't use
Their Credit Cards, Cheques and Loans,
He knew getting into debt
Would be a blunder.
He gathered all the gifts
They gave,
And with the cash
They helped him save,
He bought a mattress,
To keep his money under.

FORTY-EIGHT YEARS

For Vasili Shipilov

On the day of your arrest
The atom bomb
Was still a blackboard sketch;
Kennedy was riding
Patrol boats in the Pacific:
Churchill smoked cigars
And made history,
And Stalin said nothing
About the death of your parents.

On the day of your arrest
You were seventeen years old
And still believed
You had a future.

Forty-eight years have passed,
And the world which has turned
For others
In the tumult
Of a century of change
Has turned for you
In the certain, steady rhythms
Of confinement:

Bread and water,
Night and morning,
The sparkle of frost on stone,
The cold iron of the bars
At your window,
The constancy of hunger
In a world where imagination
Long ago gave way to routine.

And every day,
Twice a day,
Your own prayer:
Desperate and broken,
Rising with your visible breath.
A prayer for your captors
For those
Who have taken your life —
Not with the instant fury
Of bullet, noose or current,
But slowly,
Precisely,
One moment at a time.

THE GAMES PEOPLE PRAY

Some pray like a BMW:
Seven coats
Of shine and shimmer
Masking the hardness of steel,
With an Anti-Emotion Warranty
To guard against
The least sign of trust.

Some pray like a Porsche:
Nought to victory
In 6.7 seconds,
Banking on the promises
Of Pray-As-You-Earn prosperity.

Jesus recommended
Praying in the garage
With the door shut,
Engine and radio off,
Praying when no one is looking,
Forgetting
The traffic of the day.
Meeting God
In the quiet lay-by,
Far from
The Pray and Display.

THE GIFT

We were so glad to welcome him
On Christmas day:
It was like having a new member
Of the family.
He looked so small and helpless,
It made you want to pick him up
And cuddle him.
We made promises, of course,
Said we'd make room for him in our home,
Said we'd alter our routines
To fit him in,
Said we'd take a walk with him
Each day.

But the novelty
Soon began to wear off.
By New Year,
We mentioned him less often.
Daily chores were less of a thrill,
More of a reluctant duty.
By February he was unwanted.
By March we had abandoned him
Completely.

We should have read the warnings,
We should have counted the cost.
A God is for life,
Not just for Christmas.

GRAVE DECISION

They made a golf course
Of the Manor House cemetery
To bring a smile
To the tourists' faces.
Time was, it was used
To bury the rich:
Now they're putting
On heirs and Graces.

GOD IN A BOX

Anne Diamond says
You can believe what you like,
As long as you're sincere.
Russel Grant says
Your destiny
Is etched in light in the sky.
Judith Chalmers says
Life's secret lies
In wishing you were here.
Selina Scott says
You must first decide
Which designer tags to buy.
Terry Wogan says
What matters most
Is who's in, or out,
Of the News.
Alan Whicker says
It's a question
Of which plastic card you use.
They all tell you
How to think and live
And which creed
Will set you free:
It isn't only Americans
Who have evangelists
On TV.

HEALING POEM

My heart is like an iceberg.
Not cold and hard,
But seven-tenths hidden.

If I love you only
With the tenths that show,
My love won't last the course.
But if I am to love you
With my whole heart
I must face the pain
Of hidden things
Surfacing.

Come, Lord,
With the Titanic of your love.
Collide with my heart.
And in that great collision,
Let it be
My reservations
That sink for ever.

IMAGES OF SIN: GIMME, GIMME, GIMME TEMPTATION

Like a microwave oven,
It starts to cook
On the inside.
Like the small ads
In the tabloids,
It offers
What it can't provide.
Like queues
On the M25,
It brings the best plans
To a halt.
Like a badly brought up
Tennis star,
It never admits
To a fault.
Like a book club
Joined in error,
It won't let you rest
Until you're dead.
Like a topless
Liquidiser,
Its effects
Are quickly wide-spread.
Like cut-price

Plastic surgery,
Its after
Is worse than before.
Like any well-managed
Pop star,
It always leaves you
Wanting more.

Like the shepherd's
Red sky at night,
It promises delight
At sunrise.
But,
Like the sleeping dog
That it is,
It lies.

I'M GLAD

I'm glad that God
Did not so order the world
That laughter and pain
Came in separate little boxes:
Never to meet or mix.

I'm glad that the greatest comedians
Can arouse in me sadness
And anger,
And that a quadriplegic
Who paints with his teeth
And taps out prose
One letter at a time
Can teach me
The richness of comedy.

I'm glad that laughter and pain
Come intertwined
Like veins in marble:
That it takes a detective
To trace them
And poems
To root them out.

THE INVISIBLE HAND

People like a God
Who is bigger than they are:
A God whose ways are unfathomable
Shrouded in mystery
Electric with terror.
A God whom to touch is to die.
People like a God
Who looks after their interests
In return for ritualistic obedience,
Reverential fear,
And the occasional sacrifice.
A God who makes their choices for them
And justifies
The choices that they make.
People like a God
To whom they can attribute
The wealth of the wealthy
And the poverty of the poor.
A God who will ensure
That the fittest survive
And excuse the ruthless destruction
Of the unfit.

People like a God
Who rarely asks questions

And never gets too close.
A distant, inhuman
Cosmic-roulette-wheel of a God.

That's why they invented
Free Market Economics.

ISLAND LIFE

Sentenced,
In a crowded room,
To solitary confinement
We cling to our smiles
Like lifebelts
And pray
They will keep us afloat.
Like the child who drowned
In a busy swimming pool,
It isn't that no one cares
Just that no one sees
We're there.

No man is an island,
But when it comes
To making causeways
Most of us
Are all at sea.

I WONDER IF ARMS DEALERS OBJECT TO SUNDAY TRADING

Every fortnight
Twice a month,
People who are out of work
Receive a Giro:
Except those registered as vagrant
(Who have to sign on daily).
Every fortnight
Twice a month,
I consume
Approximately forty-two meals
And sleep,
If I'm lucky,
One hundred and twelve hours.
Every fortnight
Twice a month,
I use up one twenty-sixth
Of my TV licence;
Christmas
Gets twelve shopping days closer,
And one tenth of a per cent
Of my expected future
Joins
My remembered past.
And every fortnight

Twice a month,
The politicians of the world
Spend enough on arms
To feed
And clothe
And house
And educate
The population of the planet
For a year.
That's six months of poverty
For every seven days
Of trading.

No wonder they say
A week
Is a long crime in politics.

LITURGY: LET YOUR KINGDOM COME

Let it break out like blisters
On the skin of this city,
Let it cut to the heart
Like cardiac surgery.
Let it be as deeply rooted
As cedars, touching bedrock,
Let it travel more widely
Than Zaphod Beeblebrock.
Let it be more arresting
Than the Special Patrol Group,
Let it come like Hotwheels cars
Scorching down to loop the loop.
Let it spread on the grapevine
Like a death on EastEnders,
Let it cause such a stir
As a wedding on Neighbours.

Let it come like a hurricane
Like a fire, like a river,
Let it spread like a virus,
Like war, like a rumour.
Like the raising of a curtain
Like the roll of a drum,
Let it come to us,
Let your kingdom come.

Let its landing be more welcomed
Than Michael Jackson's jet,
Let it affect more households
Than the rise of credit debt.
Let it arouse greater faith
Than the Pope, kissing tarmac,
Let it come with more relish
Than Large Fries and a Big Mac.
Let it win more accolades
Than Olivier's acting,
Let it relieve suffering
More than Botha repenting.
Let it touch as many lives
As water fluoridation,
Let it seep through more frontiers
Than Chernobyl's radiation.

Let it come like a hurricane
Like a fire, like a river,
Let it spread like a virus
Like war, like a rumour.
Like the raising of a curtain
Like the roll of a drum,
Let it come to us,
Let your kingdom come.

LORD, TEACH US TO PRAY

There's only one way
To train
A decathlon champion:

Daley.

A MARVELLOUS HEALING

For John Baker

It was a marvellous healing;
After the months of asking,
Of waiting;
After the desperate, slow deterioration,
The warring tides
Of faith and doubt:
To be released, in an instant,
From every pain.
It was as if the very molecules of his flesh
Had been infused, invaded,
With the life of God,
Until he was filled, fit to burst,
With the Shalom, the peace,
Of the Father's rule.
Limbs that had fallen flaccid with weakness
Waved and danced with joy;
Lungs that had so utterly failed him
Sang out with strength and boldness.

He ran
Through the unfamiliar sunlight,
Drinking it in,
Experiencing all at once

The thousand and one feelings
That for so long had been denied him.

It was a marvellous healing:
To be so totally restored,
Made whole,
Rebuilt.
It had just surprised him,
A little,
That he had had to die
To receive it.

MERGER MANIA

If the Mormons took over
The Seventh Day Adventists,
Their expansionist zeal
Overcoming all restraints,
Would their newly merged faith
Of blue-suited evangelists
Be called the Church
Of the Saturday Saints?

MARX

I always think of Karl Marx
As in the popular photograph:
Hair shooting off
In monochrome fireworks,
The tight mouth
Engulfed
In a jungle of greying beard.

And the eyes
Fixed, straight ahead:
Judging the trivial lens,
Eyeing up
The twentieth century
For a fight.

MODERN ROMANCE

She
was a blushing English rose,
A small-town girl,
Discontented with her fate.
Believing the lie, that love had passed her by,
She wondered if she'd ever
Find a mate.

He
was straight out of an advert for Levis;
Crew-cut hair, perfect teeth,
An easy smile.
Wallet bulging in the pocket
Of his well-worn flying jacket,
A Guardian of Democracy,
American style.

They would meet
Through the wire of the perimeter fence,
She'd ignore the warnings,
Come up close, to catch his eye.
He'd volunteer regularly for additional guard duty
Without telling anyone why.

.And casting long shadows
In the halogen glare
Of the floodlights, suspended high above,
They fixed each other's gaze, and spoke of childhood
    days,
And swapped photographs,
And laughed
And fell in love.

They're married now, with kids,
And posted to Germany.
They speak of romance, but mostly in the past tense,
But they never will lose sight
Of that first, surprising night
When they met
Through the Greenham Common fence.

NEWSRAP

A fifty-year-old woman
Was assaulted today
In a car park putting
Her shopping away.
A five-year-old girl
Went missing from the park,
Police gave a warning:
Don't stray out after dark.
On the London Stock Exchange
The Pound took a dive,
But a nun in East Grinstead
Has seen Elvis Alive.
Rottweiler dogs
Have mauled another child
But the weather for the weekend
Will be sunny and mild.
And there's good news, bad news,
Banner headlines,
Cool dudes and fool nudes,
Bingo, star signs:
And in amongst the wreckage,
There's a message for today:
The world is going crazy,
That's what the papers say.
Massacres and murders

Shut-downs and strikes,
A judge into bondage
Does what he likes.
False allegations
And scandalous stories:
Thatcher blames the Reds,
The rest blame the Tories.
Insider dealing,
No one left to trust;
We paid our broker
But our broker went bust.
A vicar in Brixton
Can no longer cope:
He didn't need reporters,
What he needed was hope.
And there's good news, bad news
Banner headlines,
Cool dudes and fool nudes,
Bingo, star signs
And in amongst the wreckage
There's a message for today:
The world is going crazy,
That's what
The papers say.

PENNIES IN THE RAG PARADE

We collect pain
In buckets
Like pennies in the rag parade.
You're supposed to hand them in
At the end of the day:
Empty your bucket
At the central collecting point.

But some of us miss it,
Somehow,
And find
We have carried the pain home.
And we'd like
To give the bucket back:
But how do you explain
The pennies?

In the end we get used to it,
And the bucket
Becomes a kind of souvenir.
And the pennies?
They just sit in it.
There isn't anywhere else
To put them.

PERFORMANCE FOR AN AUDIENCE OF ONE

If you had been
The only one:
Yours the only ticket sold,
Your solitary bottom
Spoilt for choice
In an ocean of empty seats.
If you had been
The only one,
He still would have staged
The whole show.

The brooding, hovering chords
Of the overture
Would have unfolded for your ears only:
Stars spinning out like Catherine wheels
Across a dark but lightening set
Until dawn was uncorked
On green home.

Act I:
The building of a nation.
A people wooed and won
And lost
And won again.
For you alone the whole cast

Weaving and turning through dances
That fill a joyous expanse of stage.

Act II:
The cry of a child
In a vastly empty universe.
The adventure
Of hope and betrayal.
The seat-gripping climax:
Triumph diving,
Death defying
Through the fiery hoop of tragedy.
To lead into the crowd scenes
Building
Toward an unimagined finale:
A cosmos, purged of guilt,
Restored,
Dressed for dancing.

If you had been
The only one:
Your grimy pounds the total take,
He still would have staged
The whole show,
And wept for joy
At the warmth of your applause.

PITCH PERFECT

At the funeral of a child,
The mourners
Tread carefully;
Wondering whose grief
They are walking over.
The lawns are neat,
Well spaced,
Tightly turfed
In grounds as cosseted
As a First Division
Football pitch.

I break away
From the tight knot
Of suits and tears and silence,
And stand apart:
A momentary observer.
And like the ball
Of a demolition crane,
Like bricks falling,
Like the clods that thump and tumble
On the dwarfed coffin's lid,
The thought hits me:
This is not the end.

And I want to be here,
On this very spot,
In the shadow of this gothic chapel,
An observer again
Amid these geometric lawns,
On the day when the earth erupts,
And stones crack like biscuits,
And coffins splinter
Into matchwood memories.
I want to stand
On the sidelines
When the final whistle blows
And resurrection
Like a pitch invasion
Runs its wild and muddy boots
All over
Death's neat and tended
Astroturf.

POEM FOR A BORING CAREERS LESSON

A young man
With a career in design,
Felt the standard of his work
Was a sign,
That he was never designed
To design.
So, resigned to his failure,
He resigned,
And his contract to design
Was de-signed.

But a sign-writer
Who saw his designs
Saw promise
For a designer of signs,
So with his contract
Re-designed
For a career
In sign design,
The resigning designer
Re-signed.

POETIC JUSTICE

Supermarket trolley,
Oh, supermarket trolley:
Discarded and forgotten
Like an outdated song,
Do you remember the days
When, chrome-bright and jolly,
You danced like a dodgem
Through the fruit-weighing throng?

I know some would accuse me
Of sentimental folly:
But I'm sad to see the drowning
Of a supermarket trolley.

Your mesh is enmeshed now
With river-weed and slime,
And the letters on your handle
Are irreversibly smudged,
And though I could simply say
That you've fallen on hard times,
It gives me unexpected pleasure
To believe you're being judged...

For all those times,
In some crowded aisle or other,
When I pushed you one way
And your wheels
Went another.

Sick of living
In this hole:
DOLE.
Something coming
In the air:
DESPAIR.
That's the third
Demand they've sent:
RENT.
We could get three meals
Out of that:
CAT.
With this address,
You'll never get it:
CREDIT.
The only shopping
Our sort know:
WINDOW.

All the young
Can think about:
GETTING OUT.
·Don't worry love,
Somehow we'll cope:
HOPE.

PRAYER

I prayed that God would give me
A new car.
Prayed that I'd receive it
That same day.
I prayed that my hunger
For comfort and prestige,
In a moment of pure joy,
Would melt away.
At the outset of the day
And with lunch to look forward to,
I prayed
That God would give me a new car.

But instead,
He took me on a journey.
He sat me in the entrance
To a makeshift tent,
Where the ground,
And the canvas,
And my clothes,
And my skin,
Were the single, sickly
Monochrome brown
Of the dusts of drought.
The only sound

The sound of crying:
The sound of hope
Fading.
The sound of despair
Growing.
All around me
Was a sea of such tents,
An ocean of such people.
There was nothing to look forward to
But sixteen daylight hours of this,
Each one the hour
In which my children would ask
For the food I could not provide.
Sixteen hours,
And at day's end,
The hope of sleep.
And at the end of the last day,
When that would come,
The hope of a painless death.

At the outset of the day
With lunch to look forward to,
I prayed
That God would give me
A new car.
And I, for one,
Am glad that he said no.

PRISONER OF CONSCIENCE

I cannot tell
How it might feel
To wake each morning to
The icing silence
Of four stone walls as
Familiar as a hutch to a rabbit.
To have the routines of my life
Reduced
To patterns traced
And mindlessly retraced
On twelve square feet
Of dirty concrete.

I do not know
What it is
For those who are closest to me to be
Furthest away
And for two feet of brick,
A bullet-guarded compound,
And sixty years of judicial abuse
To come between.

I cannot know
What putrid cabbage
Floating in a soup as thin as mist

Might taste like
In the fifteenth winter
Of near starvation.

There is nothing
In the lexicon of my experience
To give flesh to such ideas:
On the gallery walls
Of my memory
These pictures have no place.
But I do know that there are
Thousands who have lived
And died this way:
And that but for accident
Of birth they might be me.
And I know
That if I was, truly,
A prisoner of my conscience,
I would by now
Have been more deeply moved.

PROGRESS REVISITED

If a Reverend,
Promoted to Bishop,
Becomes a Right Reverend,
And if an Honourable Member
On appointment to the Privy Seal
Becomes a Right Honourable Member,
Does a State
Increasingly centrally governed
Eventually get into
A right state?

PROSPERITY GOSPEL

It's the Gospel
To end all grieving,
The joy
To end all sorrows,
The ultimate
Reward for believing:

For they that sow in tithes
Shall reap in Volvos.

PUSH-BUTTON CENSOR

You can always switch it off,
They said,
When you can't take any more.
If a scene is explicit
And you think you should miss it:
That's what the on/off switch is for.

So
When horror and death filled the screen,
I let my finger prove
My right to choose.
And when the carnage had gone,
I thought,
I'll just switch back on
When they've finished
Reading the News.

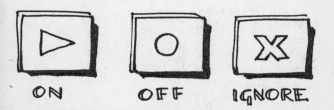

ON   OFF   IGNORE

A QUESTION OF VALUES

It's a question of values
Says the Company Director
As he signs the last redundancies
And saves the car
For another month.

It's a question of values
As we pass around
The seconds of roast
While Ethiopia dies slowly
On the Sunday News.

It's a question of values
When the old die
Cold and alone
Because families
Didn't have the time.

It's a question of values
You know I'd do more
Give more
Care more,
But first let me
Bury my father
Tend to my business

Take a well-earned holiday
Look to my career....

If your heart is where your treasure is
Then mine
Is on deposit on the High St.,
Bonus Interest
And Seven Days' notice
Of withdrawal.

Was it a question of values
For God
As he looked on a world
Sick with selfishness
Bent on destruction
Corrupt and dying:
As he weighed up the worth
Of worthless man
And considered him
Worth dying for?

RAPTURE RAP

A Poem for Two Voices

One: West is best
Forget the rest
We've marked the East
With the number of the Beast.
It really doesn't matter
If the innocent are captured:
When the going gets tough
The saved get RAPTURED!

Bush is in the Whitehouse
Finger on the button,
Black kids are starving,
White man's a glutton.
Who cares about the soul,
When the dollar's in control?
You can't stop the party
Once the music starts to roll.

Two: Down in South America
Civil war rages,
Contras do the fighting
Senate pays the wages.
Drummers drumming
Choppers humming:

Go tell Olly
Armageddon's coming.

Together: West is best
Forget the rest
We've marked the East
With the number of the Beast.
It really doesn't matter
If the innocent are captured:
When the going gets tough
The saved get RAPTURED!

Two: Preachers preach
One: A gospel of prosperity
Two: Teachers teach
One: Suspicion of austerity
Two: Don't worry about the poor
Or the beggar at your door
If you let him in
He'll only mess
The carpet on your floor.

One: Got no fears
For the future of the Nation
Two: We're on the winning side
In the Book of Revelation
One: We've tithed our dues
We just can't lose,
Together: It won't be us singing
The LEFT BEHIND BLUES.

Together: West is best, etc.

REFLECTION

I used to think my parents
Had always wanted a girl:
But it was just
A mis-conception.

THE SKIN OF A STRANGER

There is a skin that is not
The skin of a stranger.
There is a touch
That can catch her
On the ragged edge of fear.
There is a breath
That breathes so closely
It mixes with her own.
There is a voice
That she knows
And she knows should not be here.

Salt to the wound, he asks,
Do you love me?
And turns a key in the lock
Of the cell
That he has built.
Misguiding her loyalty
He swears her to secrecy;
She falls into his darkness,
An uninvited guilt.

There is a game
She's learnt to play:
Conspiracy of Silence.

She is an exile,
Looking homeward
From her own twilight zone.
No one's going to reach her
Touch her
Know her
Hurt her:
The only safe bet
Is that you're safer alone.

And who is going to teach her
To trust
In the power of love
When trust
Has taught her only
How to cry?
And who is going to show her
The truth
Of a father's love
When it's her father
Who has shown her the lie?

SMALL CHANGE

Money changes hands,
They say,
And its habit
Is to change them into fists.

SPIKE MILLIGAN SAYS IT'S NATURE'S WAY
OF TELLING US TO SLOW DOWN

Spike Milligan says
It's nature's way
Of telling us to slow down.
Like the best
Of Chopin's sonatas,
It always comes packaged
In silence.
Even when there are screams
And gun fire
And engines falling
Out of the sky,
The silence swallows them
Like an ocean
Engulfing wreckage.
Like furniture moved
After many years,
It is marked
By an outline around vacated space.
Like distance it brings a change
To the significance of photographs.
Like a night on the tiles,
The real pain
Is in the mourning after....

Like Coca-Cola,
Mickey Mouse,
Encyclopedias
And Life Insurance,
It is a universally available product.
And though we do our best
To dodge its salesmen,
In the end
We all buy it.

SOUTH AFRICA

In South Africa
God sends the sun
To shine on the just
And the unjust alike.

Problem is,
The unjust
Have got all the parasols.

SURVIVAL DAY

It should have been
A more momentous occasion.
There should have been some act,
Some symbol,
To mark the moment when you passed
From tenuous anonymity
To the legal certainty of personhood.
When you inherited
The protection of the living,
And crossed the boundary
Between merciful destruction
And murder.

There should have been a ceremony
To herald your survival.

But there was
No ceremony,
There were no crowds,
No telegrams were sent.
No one even noticed
When the first day of your 29th week began
Just as the last of your 28th had ended:
With the furious rushing of blood,
The racing of your pulse,

And the constant, soporific rhythm
Of that other heart, beating.

The gentle, amber light
Of life.
The soft, lapping fluid
Of safety.

A THEOLOGIAN LOOKS
AT TOWER BLOCK DESIGN

In the Creation,
We see how God,
In six days out of seven,
Lifts order out of chaos.

In the Fall,
We find that six days
Out of every seven
Are chaos,
Since the lifts are out of order.

THREE KINGS AND A BABY

Three kings and a baby
Caught in a stable:
A moment, frozen for all time,
On a small square
Of crinkle-cut card.
The rich blue
Of the Bethlehem sky
Bleeds out at the edge,
Where a few tenacious grains
Of glitter
Cling to one
Outsized star.

They weren't, of course,
Kings.
More likely astrologers,
Scholars anyhow.
And he wasn't a baby:
Well past 18 months
When they came.

Makes you wonder
What happened to the gifts?
The gold would have been useful:
Plenty to save for

In a young family, setting out.
But what of Frankincense
And Myrrh,
The perfume of royalty,
The spice of burials.
Hardly the most suitable of gifts
For a toddler
Just out of nappies.

Chances are
They would have stayed around the house:
Conversation pieces
In their finely carved boxes.
Their symbols
Of a strange and distant land,
Like photographs
Of long-dead relatives,
Must have fed the curiosity
Of an exploring, inquisitive child.
He must have looked at them,
Held them, sometimes,
Wondered at their mystery.

And did he leave them
At his mother's house,
On the day that he walked away?
And did she
Bring them with her,
Under the falling darkness
Of that Friday sky,
To a tomb in the garden

Of another Joseph,
To break open the seals
Of thirty years,
To set free the fragrances
Of burial and kingship:
And the memory
Of the men who once came
To share their proof
That what she knew
Was true.

TRANSPORTS OF DELIGHT

If a transplant
Is science changing hearts
And transport
Is people changing places
Then a leopard
Changing spots
Ought to be a simple matter
Of trans-fur.

THE TRIALS OF THE UPWARDLY MOBILE

The trouble with having
A new filofax
With its pages
And pages
And pages
Is that thinking of things
To fill them all with
Takes ages
And ages
And ages.
So you buy maps of places
You'll never go,
And charts for conversions
You've no reason to use,
And you list all the people
You hardly know,
And the numbers of hotels
Too pricey to choose.
And when you've facted
And filed to the max,
And entered it all,
Without restriction:
What you're left with is less
Of a filofax,
More
Of a filofiction.

THE TROUBLE WITH REALITY

The trouble with reality
Is that if you miss it
There's no Omnibus Edition
To help you catch up.
The trouble with reality
Is that you can't video it
While you're out at the pub,
And fast-forward
Through the highlights
Over a hot cup of cocoa.
The trouble with reality
Is that when your friends die
They don't pop back
In the next series
To tell you
It was all a bad dream.
The trouble with reality
Is that the Casting Director
Never consults you
Before choosing
The people next door.
The trouble with reality
Is that it's easier
To watch Neighbours
Than to be one.

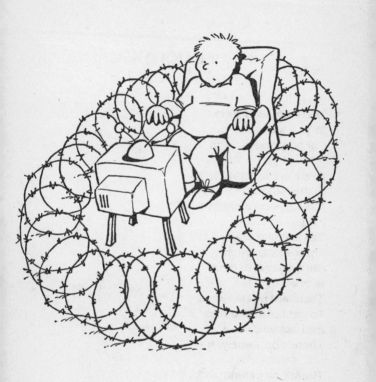

UNIQUE

There are ten letters
In 'population',
But only one of them
Is U.
There are several Starks
In the Nation,
But only one of them
Is Koo.
Call My Bluff offers
Three explanations,
But only one of them
Is true.
There are no two ways
To get through a maze
And likewise
There's only one you.

There's one Mona Lisa,
One Robin Hood,
There's only one
QE II.
Though others share
The Hundred Acre Wood,
There's only one
Winnie-the-Pooh.

And while some spies search
For a gadgeteer as good,
For James Bond
There's only one Q.
There's one Nina Ricci,
One Mouse that's Mickey,
And it's tricky,
But there's only one you.

Roses are red,
Violets are blue,
Genetics have proved it:
There's only
One you.

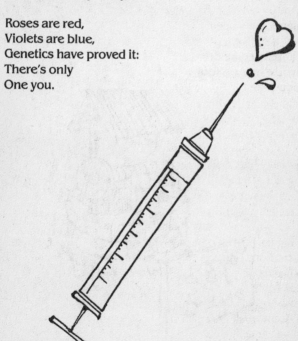

VERSERY RHYME

Jack and Jill
Went up the hill
To sup
Their local's beer.
Jack had five,
But insisted he drive,
So now he's on foot
For a year.

120

VICIOUS CIRCLE DANCE

CRY
Is what the child in me
Will do
When he feels that he can't
COPE
Is what the adult does
When he feels he shouldn't
CRY
Is what I sometimes do
When I can no longer
COPE
With deciding
Whether to cope or cry.

WORDS: A POET'S POEM

I used to
PASSWORDS
By, without a second glance.
Even when I came a
CROSSWORDS
I had never met before,
I rarely took the time
To get acquainted.
Sometimes I would
CATCHWORDS
Trying to sneak up on me,
But I never let them get
The upper hand.

But just lately
I have been enthralled
BYWORDS
They entice and ensnare me;
They take hold of my attention
At the most inconvenient
Of moments.
If I were more
WISE WORDS
Wouldn't have
This power over me.

But since I find it
So hard to be
STRONG WORDS
Very often get the better of me:
I am defenceless, I
SWEARWORDS
Will be my downfall.

YOUTH ON THE DOLE

TIME is MONEY

They gave him more than he knew how to fill,
   And never enough to fill it.
They said that at least he had some on his hands,
   Even though there was none in his pocket.
They told him if only he would use it constructively,
   Very soon, he'd learn to manage without it.
But he found a way of making some quickly:
   And wound up with them
   Making him do it.

Clearing Away The Rubbish

by Adrian Plass

How we love to make life complicated! So much of what we do looks worth while, but unless its roots are in Reality it's just another piece of rubbish.

Through humour, poetry, songs and drama. Adrian Plass invites us to clear away the rubbish that our Infernal Enemy delights in tipping into our lives.

ADRIAN PLASS is well known for his ability to strip away the veneer of hypocrisy of super-spirituality that bedevils so many of us. Many of these pieces—ideal for amateur performance—will encourage us to rediscover an uncluttered pathway to the truth.

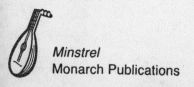

Minstrel
Monarch Publications

Monarch Publications

Monarch Publications was founded to produce books from a Christian perspective which challenge the way people think and feel. Our books are intended to appeal to a very wide constituency, in order to encourage Christian values which currently seem to be in decline.

Monarch Publications has three imprints:

<u>Monarch</u> is concerned with issues, to develop the mind.

<u>MARC</u> is a skills-based list, concentrating on leadership and mission.

<u>Minstrel</u> concentrates on creative writing, to stimulate the imagination.

Monarch Publications is owned by The Servant Trust, a Christian charity run by representatives of the evangelical church in Britain, committed to serve God in publishing and music.

For further information on the Trust, including details of how you may be able to support its work, please write to:

> The Secretary
> The Servant Trust
> 1 St Anne's Road
> Eastbourne
> East Sussex BN21 3UN
> England